GOD ONLY KNOWS

POEMS OF LOVE, DEPRESSION, HOPE, NATURE, STRESS AND CATHARTIC WRITING

CLAUS RANSWILL

LIGHT SWITCH
PRESS

Published by:
Light Switch Press
PO Box 272847
Fort Collins, CO 80527

Copyright © Claus Ranswill 2020

ISBN: 978-1-949563-93-1

Printed in the United States of America

No part of this publication may be reproduced, stored in a retrieval system, or transmitted in any form or by any means – electronic, mechanical, digital photocopy, recording, or any other without the prior permission of the author.

All rights reserved solely by the author. The author guarantees all contents are original and do not infringe upon the legal rights of any other person or work. The views expressed in this book are not necessarily those of the publisher.

TABLE OF CONTENTS:

WHY AND HOW THIS BOOK CAME TO BE	1
I WOULD LIKE TO THANK GOD	3
DREAMGIRL	4
MY LOVE MY LIFE	5
LOOK INTO MY EYES	7
GIRL	8
THE LOVE IS OVER?	9
THE BEST DAY	10
OPEN YOUR HEART	11
SOCIAL MISFITS	12
JUST BECAUSE	13
EVERYTIME	14
WHAT IS THIS LIFE	15
CONDITIONAL LOVE	17
DEBBIE	18
DON'T SAY IT	19
DRIVING TOO FAST	21
EASTER AND CHRISTMAS DISGUISED	22
EDUCATION IS A PROCESS	23
FOREVER AND A DAY	24
I DON'T KNOW	25
LOVE IS LIKE A PRISON	27
LOVE	28
MY LOVE IS FOREVER	29
MY IDEAL MATE	30
OPPOSITES ATTRACT	31
THE LONELY REACH	32

THE PRISONER OF LOVE	33
YOU DON'T LOVE ME	34
YOU GIVE MEANING TO MY LIFE	35
ANXIETY AND DEPRESSION	36
CALL ME LAZY	37
CAN YOU RELATE	38
CAN'T STOP	39
CAN'T HELP IT	40
CAN'T SLEEP	41
DEPRESSION	42
SENSITIZATION	43
DISORGANIZATION	44
FORGIVENESS	45
FREEDOM OF SPEECH	46
FREEDOM	47
GODS CREATURES	48
HE PICKED THE ROAD LESS TRAVELED BY	49
HOLLANDS THEMES	50
HOW LONG HAVE I?	51
I CANNOT	52
I DON'T HAVE TIME	53
I LOVE THE NIGHT	54
I WONDER HOW MANY	55
IF ONLY I COULD	56
IF ONLY I HAD	57
IMAGINATION	58
IMMORALITY	59
INSPIRATION NOT PERSPIRATION	60
IT'S BEEN A WHILE	61
LET ME DESCRIBE WHAT IT'S LIKE	62

LETTING OFF STEAM	63
LIFE CAN BE COMPLICATED	64
LIFE IS SO TOUGH	65
LIFE	66
LIGHT	68
LITTLE BY LITTLE	69
LOW SELF-ESTEEM	70
MONEY	71
MORE MONEY	72
NEVER ENOUGH MONEY	73
NEVER LIVED IN THE HOOD	74
NEVER TO SURRENDER	75
OLD SAYINGS	76
ONE DAY CLOSER	77
ONE DAY SITTING	78
ONE TWO	79
ONE – TWO - THREE	80
STORY OF MY LIFE	81
SUICIDE IS NO ANSWER	83
SUNSET BY THE BEACH	85
TELEVISION	86
TEN YEARS WASTED	87
THE SADDEST DAY	89
THE SIMPLE CHORES OF LIFE	90
THOUGHTS	91
TIME IS FAST	92
TIME IS TOO SHORT	93
TIME	94
TOBACCO COMPANY OWNERS	95
TOBACCO EXECS	96

TOO MANY PEOPLE	97
UNCONTROLLABLE	98
VANITY	99
WHAT IS A POEM	100
WHAT IS IN THE AIR	101
WHAT ARE WE	102
WHAT DOES IT TAKE	103
WHEN I SIT DOWN TO WRITE	104
WHO KNOWS WHAT?	105
WHY I CREATE ART	106
WHY NOT BELIEVE?	107
WHY, WHY, WHY?	108
WHY	109
WRITING	110
WROTE ANOTHER POEM	111
YESTERDAY IS FOREVER GONE	112
TODAY, TOMORROW, OR YESTERDAY	113
YOU DON'T UNDERSTAND	114
LONG JOURNEY IN MY MIND	115

WHY AND HOW THIS BOOK CAME TO BE

The following poems, lyrics, and words were written from 2000 to 2003. Some have been placed in books, booklets, songs and now this book. I would first like to thank God for giving me this gift for writing that I didn't know I had until 2000 when I was attending our local community college, College of the Desert. I think these are some of my best poems, I tried to pick 100 of the best ones to put into this book. They are in no particular order.

Some of these poems were written because of assignments from college professors at COD, college of the desert. Some came about due to stress, love, anxiety, and thoughts of life. Some came about from suggestions.

I would also like to thank my beautiful wife Debbie for standing by me through thick and thin, rich and poor, highs and lows. She has been the inspiration for many of these poems. I would also like to thank my children, family, and in laws for their love, affection, and encouragement.

I would also like to thank all my teachers and professors in my college classes, they were encouraging and very helpful with my growth in writing. Some of the main professors were Mr. Ted Grofer, Mr. Terry Nicholson, Mr. Jack Tapleshay, and Ms. Ruth Nolan and Ms. Amy Dibello just to name a few. All the professors were great and all the education I have received has helped me become who I am today.

It is much easier to sit and watch television than to go through a folder full of files of poems and lyrics and trying to decide which ones deserve to be in this book, and which ones will have to wait until the next book to be seen and read.

Some of my poems feel like songs, some are just cathartic, and others range from love, depression, anger, nature, and life in general. Some don't rhyme and some are kind of strange, but all are from the heart and gifted to me from God.

To all readers, thank you for buying, reading, enjoying, and sharing. My only wish is for everyone to enjoy at least one of them and share it with another.

Remember you don't have to love all of my poems, but if you love at least one, that would be great. Just like rock n roll or county music, not all songs from a band are good, but some are really great. Thanks for reading and please let everyone know about this book.

I WOULD LIKE TO THANK GOD

I would like to thank GOD
for the gift I didn't know I had
Until I was fired from my job
then became really sad.

I soon became a full time student
at our local college C.O.D.
At the end of the week
my energy's spent.
Taking six classes
still don't know what I want to be.

I would like to thank
my acting teacher Terry Nicholson,
for giving me the assignment
of writing five poems.
One day I sat down, wrote ten
and guess who's my Inspiration.
My beautiful wife Debbie,
and my children Aaron, Joshua, and Kirsten

DREAMGIRL

Girl of my dreams
Woman of desire
You give me the feelings
of burning fire

Girl of desire
Woman of my dreams
Fuel the fire
like long running streams

Girl of my dreams
Woman of desire
Beautiful long streams
of colorful fire

Dreaming of the girl
Desiring all the while
Looking like a pearl
Every time that she smiles

Diamond in the rough
Precious metal gold
She is always tough
Forever-young, never old

MY LOVE MY LIFE

You are my love.
You are my life.
You're the gift from above,
That became my wife.
Love of my life,
Mother of my children.
You are my wife,
Sent from heaven.

Sixteen years.
That's a mighty long time.
Many, many, tears.
Together till the end of time.
Looking towards the future.
Can't forget the past.
Everyday we become more mature,
I know our love will last.

Me and you forever,
Till death do us part.
These words will last forever.
Nothing can tear us apart.

For richer and for poorer.
I know we've had our share.
It always seems to be poorer.
Sometimes we cannot bear.

I know its temporary.
Won't last too much longer.
The riches will make us very,
Overwhelmingly stronger.

Take these words and keep them,
Close to your heart.
Never to forget them,
Then we can start,
To live happily forever.
Together till the end.
Never will we waiver,
Never will we bend.

LOOK INTO MY EYES

Look into my eyes--- tell me what you see
Is it a normal guy---or is it insanity
Trying to dwell ---inside my brain
Starting to swell---causing too much pain

Look into my eyes---what do you see now
Thin white disguise---bet you don't know how
To control your feelings---locked up deep inside
Instead you start reeling---then run away and hide

Take control ---of the situation
Remain in control ---don't give in to temptation
Look into my soul---deep desperation
Deep inside my soul---flirting with salvation

Longing for love---look into my eyes
You can be my dove---spread your wings and fly
God from up above---if I will only try
To give all my love---he will pull me into the sky

Then I can live in eternity---
With fallen loved ones up in heaven
Where we all can be
Finally free
Of all this insanity

GIRL

Girl, you are so beautiful
Girl, you are my queen
Girl, you make my life so full
Even when you're mean

Girl, you make my life complete
Every time I think of you
There's no other girl I need to meet
Now that I've met you

There is only one girl for me
That would be you
There is nothing I need to be
Now that I have you

There is no one else for me
Since you're in my life
There could never ever be
Another girl for my wife

Girl, you are the one for me
I hope you feel the same
Girl these words are all from me
I hope you don't think they are too lame

Girl, these words are from the heart
I hope you still believe
Girl, I hope one-day you'll start
Then you will conceive

THE LOVE IS OVER?

The love is over between you and me.
Forever I thought it would last, how could this be?
The love is over between me and you.
Now I don't know what else I can do.
Without you love in my life,
I'll live forever till eternity in strife.
Forever I thought it would never end.
Forever I thought, we would always send,
Our love to each other and no one else.
How could our love end up on the shelf?
Empty and alone, that's all I feel.
Another moment of love, I wish I could steal,
From you and maybe change your mind.
Another moment of love, won't you be so kind?
To give me just another chance,
To show my love and maybe enhance,
Your love for me then maybe you'll change,
Your mind about love and stretch the range,
Of love between me and you.
I know it's something you can do.

THE BEST DAY

The best day of my life changes everyday.
The worst day of my life I know will never stay,
in my memory and in my brain.
If I think too hard, I'll start to strain.

I cannot remember the feelings that I had.
I cannot remember being happy or even sad.
Past moments, I try to hide.
I bury the feelings deep down inside.

The best day--- the worst day,
sometimes they intertwine.
The worst day--- the best day,
at least I know they're mine.

One day soon, I hope to remember.
I try to think back to that day in September.
My whole life changed, I thought for the worst.
It was only for the best, now my life has a thirst.

You never know what life has in store.
You never know what is exciting and what is a bore.
A single moment in time, it happened so fast.
Now I can't believe, my life is such a blast.

OPEN YOUR HEART

Open your heart---let me in.
Don't shut me out---let me begin,
to show you my love---that is eternal,
don't put me through---this hellish inferno.

Open your heart---let me begin,
to show you my love---that is within,
my heart and soul---my body and mind,
I'll give it all---and I won't look behind.

I'll give it all---to you my love,
I'll make you feel---like heaven above.

Open your heart---let me in,
then you can start---and we can begin,
to share our love---and all our affection,
like a little white dove---they'll be no need for correction.

Open your heart---let me in,
then we can start---then we can win.

SOCIAL MISFITS

Social misfits, outcasts are we all.
Who will catch us when we fall?
Overbearing senses of trying to crawl.
No questions from us are too small.

Feelings of devotion from up above,
Overpowers us all, complete with his love.
Whether you believe, even if you don't.
No way to control even if you won't,
Acknowledge his existence,
Pray for persistence,
Then you will receive his ever-loving assistance.

I'm not perfect, and neither are you.
We try to do the best that we can,
With each new day bringing new things to do,
Trying to please GOD the best that we can.

Don't be a hypocrite, just be yourself.
Don't let your life end up on the shelf.
With nothing worthwhile to remember you by.
If your life becomes a waste, GOD will truly cry.

JUST BECAUSE

Just because I love you
Just because the sky is blue
Just because our love is true
Just because it's between me and you

Me and you our love will grow
You and me the love will flow
Just because we're together
Our love is lighter than any feather

Just because I say it's true
It's like a picture I just drew
That's the way it's got to be
Like the flower and the tree

Paint a picture of our love
Just because it's from above
The love between us will forever grow
Always fast and never slow

The love we have will last forever
No matter how much people say never
No one can ever tear us in two
Just because it's between me and you

Just because we are together
That is why we will forever
Be together for eternity
Just because it's you and me

EVERYTIME

Everytime I close my eyes
and try to fall asleep.
These words seem to materialize
appearing just like sheep.

They don't want to go away.
They seem to fill my brain.
They don't know whether to leave or stay.
They're driving me insane.

So many words, so little time.
So many rhythms, so many rhymes.

Close my eyes, I try to sleep.
Can't here a sound, not even a peep.
No one awake no one around.
All these words make such a loud sound.

I try to remember, hope not to forget.
So I open my eyes, grab pen, paper and let,
all the words and all the emotion,
flow on to the paper, like a beautiful ocean.

Sometimes I never know when to end.
Sometimes I might go on too long.
All I know is that I want to send,
a message to the world in a beautiful song.

WHAT IS THIS LIFE

What is this life ---which we all lead?
Into my brain---I feel the stampede
Of depression, anxiety, anger and more.
What does my life ---now have in store?

I can't imagine ---I want so much
Material belongings---because they are such.
Beautiful and meaningful---I think they'll give me life.
Besides my two boys, my daughter, and my wife.

What is this life ---that I am leading?
People drive so slow---they make it look like I'm speeding.
I try to forget the past---trying to look forward.
How much longer will it last---will I be able to move forward.

What is this life---which we try to lead?
Does it matter our religion, beliefs, or creed?
Do we all have the same chance to succeed?
Or are some of us born to lose, while others born to lead?

So many questions ---it seems that's all I am.
Too much information---I always try to cram.
Into my brain---until there's no more room.
Then I write a poem, of all my anger and my gloom.

Closed My Eyes Again

Closed my eyes again---tried to sleep some more.
Words inside my brain ---knocking on the door.
If I answer---I'll have to wake up.
Get pen and paper---to shut the words up.
If I close my eyes---the words will appear.
Trampling over each other inside---my head from ear to ear.
So tired ---all I want to do is sleep.
The words are wired---they just want to keep.
Me awake---so I can write.
Like an earthquake ---words scrambling to excite.
I give up ---I'm tired of fighting.
I'll wake up--- and start to writing.
Another word---another sentence.
Another poem---is my penance.
I love to write---but also love to sleep.
I don't want to fight --- so I'll write this poem for you to keep.
Close to your heart---or inside your brain.
So I can start---to sleep and maintain.
All my energy---and all my composure.
Wrote another poem---now I have closure.

CONDITIONAL LOVE

Conditional love is all you have for me.
Why does it like that have to be?
Getting mad at me for yelling at the kids!
And not having enough patience and blowing my lid.
So easy to give up, why are you like that?
You need some patience and that is that!
Throw it all away in a single moment.
What about the happy times that we have spent?
Together so long I know I can't go on.
I'm not like you; I'm not that strong.
Where's all the kisses and all the hugs?
All I get from you is silence and a bunch of shrugs.
It used to be so nice, so fresh and new.
Where did it go? In the wind is that where it blew?
Never to be seen again, is that how you want it?
I'll never give up your love; don't you get it?
I'd rather die than live without you.
Why can't you believe these words are true?
Why else would I write, it's all for you.
All my love, I give it all to you.

DEBBIE

Debbie my love, Debbie so true,
all of my love, I give it to you.
I know it gets real hard for you.
My lack of patience makes you blue.

You don't know, how hard it is for me.
Maybe one day, you'll be able to see,
the pain that lingers inside of me.
You really think it's easy to be me?

You think I get angry on purpose?
You think I can control it?
My life has no purpose,
without you in it.

You call me an A-hole,
over and over again.
You think I can control,
my anger and my pain?

If you only knew,
the anger inside of me,
then it could be true,
the love you had for me.

You think getting a job is so easy,
finding what I like to do.
There is nothing out there for me,
that I ever want to do.

DON'T SAY IT

Don't say you don't love me.
Don't tell me that we're through.
Don't say you don't need me.
Don't make me feel so blue.

Don't say you don't love me.
Don't tell me that's it's over.
Don't tell me that you're leaving me.
Please just come on over.

Don't tell me that we're through.
Don't tell me it's the end.
Don't tell me that, you just grew.
And don't have love to send.

Don't tell me that's it's over.
Don't tell me you don't care.
Don't tell me to move on over.
This pain I cannot bare.

Don't tell me it's the end.
Don't tell me there's no more love.
Don't tell me you won't bend.
I pray to the lord above.

Don't tell me you don't care.
Don't tell me there's no more.
Don't tell me you won't share,
your love with me anymore.

Don't tell me you don't need me.
Don't tell me you don't care.
Don't tell me you don't love me.
I still have love to share.

Don't say that you don't love me.
Don't tell me that's it's true.
Don't tell me there will never be,
any more love, between me and you.

DRIVING TOO FAST

I am writing a new poem---almost every day
It's almost like a ritual---that comes into play
Whenever I start to think---my mind starts to wonder
Before I can even blink---there's a spell that I'm under

Always making mistakes---and always driving too fast
Knowing what is at stake---my license might not last

If I ever got pulled over---for doing seventy in a forty
What is my excuse---my car is too fast and just too sporty

I cannot help it--- the way that I drive
I know sometimes I'm lucky---just to be alive

I just love the adrenaline rush---that I always get
You can't even imagine---the records that I must've set

Getting here or getting there--- or nowhere in particular
You wouldn't even believe ---the times have been so spectacular

I don't even care where I am going---it doesn't really matter
No matter where I am going---people in front of me start to scatter

I don't feel too guilty---I think it's all hereditary
You should drive with my mom---her driving is way more scary

EASTER AND CHRISTMAS DISGUISED

Easter and Christmas are religious holidays,
Disguised by so much materialistic glaze.
Anything good that happens in the world,
the devil overshadows it with fake joy for boys and girls.

Take Jesus' birthday what we know as Christmas,
Satan with his power invents Santa Claus.
Then there is Easter and Jesus' resurrection,
Satan comes up with rabbits with furry little paws.

Anything GOD does Satan tries to undo,
foolish human mortals fall into this pool,
of happy gift giving days off from work,
Satan in the corner watching with a smirk.

So easy humans, fall into this trap,
Idolatry worshiping is so much crap.
Why are we, so too blind to see,
that GOD truly loves you and me?

Open your eyes, don't give in to this temptation.
Satan loves to see us in all our desperation.
Spending all our money, driving up inflation.
Give all your love to GOD; he is your only true salvation.

EDUCATION IS A PROCESS

Education is a continuing process,
Something we take for granted.
There is always information for us to access,
As long as we learn where we're planted.

Our brains are the bucket,
We fill with information.
Sometimes the words get stuck in it,
The process is assimilation.

Words are ignited into thoughts and feelings.
How we use them in a sentence,
Is how they come across in life's dealings.
Writing another poem seems to be my penance.

Once we start the education classes,
We always try to keep up with the masses.
It is a never-ending journey sometimes fast sometimes slow,
But whatever we learn, we can use it wherever we go.

Education and school were the last things on my mind.
But now that I am here I have become a bit more kind.
My brain is more open to new ideas.
My thought process is becoming a little more clear.

When we start to learn,
Our brain gets set on fire.
The more we learn,
Our IQ gets higher and higher.

This may not be what you're looking for,
But when I start to write, a poem is in store.
A drop in the bucket, another page,
Words are information and my brain is the stage.

FOREVER AND A DAY

Forever and a day
Till there is nothing left to say
Forever and a night
Love is a beautiful sight
Forever and a week
Even though life at times seems bleak

Forever my love to you
There is no more I can do
Forever my love I give
There is no other way I can live
Forever my love so true
These words I give to you
Forever my love believe
These words you can always retrieve

Forever you can keep
These words are so deep
Forever you can find
My love for you so kind
Forever you are my love
My gift from up above

I DON'T KNOW

I don't know where I am going
I don't know where I've been
I don't know how I am doing
I don't know if it's a sin

I don't know much of anything
I don't know up from down
I don't know how to dance or sing
I don't know if this will give you a frown

I don't know why I am crazy
I don't know why I am lazy
I don't know why I love to write
I don't know why I hate to fight

I don't know if I am real
I don't know what is fake
I don't know how to appeal
I don't know what is at stake

I don't know many people
I don't know why it is
I don't know much about a churches steeple
I don't know if I hit or miss

I don't know why I rhyme
I don't know if it is just me
I don't know if it is a crime
I don't know what you will see

I don't know when to end
I don't know when I've gone too long
I don't know where to begin
I don't know if I sound very strong

I don't know are three simple words
I don't know can mean so much
I don't know are more than just words
I don't know can be such a crutch

LOVE IS LIKE A PRISON

Love is like a prison.
You can't break free of its cell.
One day you feel like heaven.
The next day feels like hell.

Love is like a prison.
Isolated and all alone.
Sometimes neither rhyme nor reason.
Arguing in such a loud tone.

Love is like a prison.
You can't break free from its spell.
Once it's got you reeling
The door is locked to your cell.

Love is like a prison.
You never can escape.
Once you think you've learned your lesson,
It's erased just like videotape.

Love is like a prison.
I'm the prisoner of love.
Next time I see the sun,
I'll thank God from up above.

LOVE

Love comes to all, sometimes only once
Sometimes to others never at all
Sometimes our love makes us fall
Head over heals and we feel like a dunce

Love comes to some maybe two or three times
Others never at all it can be such a crime
Enjoy what love you get you don't know when it will end
What is important is the love you do send

Enjoy the love you get and remember it well
It can end so fast you never can tell
Ponder and think of the words I write
Before the love you have has turned to blight

Love comes to some so many times it is not fair
While others love life's are filled with despair
Enjoy what love you have before it's too late
And the love you have has become opposite of great

Love comes to some so very easy
For others it's tougher than hell
Love can sometimes be mistaken for sleazy
When your love is up for sale

MY LOVE IS FOREVER

This is my song of love I give to you
Every ounce of love, through and through
I give it all, I can't hold back
It might even give me a heart attack

All my love, I give it to you
No one else could ever out do
My love for you, even though at times
I know you get tired of all my rhymes

I love you with all my heart
All you have to do is let me start
To show my love, I have for you
There's nothing else, you'll ever have to do

A love for you, a love till the end
A love forever, I will always send
To you my love, forever so true
My love is forever, so deep in love with you

You are my one and only love
There is no doubt, you were sent from up above
You are my life, my love so true
There is no one else in this world but you

There is nothing else to say
Except I'll love you forever and a day

MY IDEAL MATE

My ideal mate is the one that I've got
Wish I could say I'm happy 24 hours a day, but I'm not
Take the good with the bad
Sometimes happy, sometimes sad

Soul mates, it seems the two of us are
Her beauty radiates even from afar
I can't imagine being with another
Starting over now, would be such a bother

Together so long we still aren't perfect
But we, still together, like hand and glove fit
Sometimes our patience is worn really thin
When we start pointing out each other's sin

The children we have together, they are such a blessing
We never would have had, if we would have kept on missing
Each other on the phone, or in some of the classes
Or even at work avoiding all of our lame passes

My ideal mate, the wife I have right now
Is responsible for a lifetime of happiness to me somehow
Sooner or later we will finally click
Together overcoming financial woes I know we can lick

Together forever, together till the end
This is the message to her, my ideal mate that I will send

OPPOSITES ATTRACT

Opposites attract, why is that so?
Opposites attract. Why? I don't know.
Twinkling of an eye, glimpse across the room.
Thoughts of happiness overcoming gloom.
Has it ever happened, love at first sight?
Love is in the air, until your first fight.

Reality sets in, where do you go from here?
Love takes over, even after your first tear.

Can you get along; is there anything the same?
Since the first day, of your opening line so lame.

Is anything still common, two to three months down the road?
Sometimes you wonder,
 If the prince or princess was really a toad?

No way to know, since love is in the air.
All the happy times, in the future you will share.

Try to look back, what has happened to you?
Opposites attracted,
Love took over you!

THE LONELY REACH

Reached over to give her a kiss
I was too slow, so I had to miss
Another moment of love and affection
What is the cause of all this misdirection?

Tried to slip in and give her a hug
All she did was give me a shrug
Pushed away and made me so sad
How much longer before I become glad

Too much pushing and shoving
Driving me away with no loving
Feelings of devotion and tenderness
What happened to all the sweetness?

Vanished into the past
How long can the pain last
Heart is broken and full of pain
Another year might drive me insane

No reason for this lack of devotion
What she needs is a lot of love lotion
To prove the feelings I have for her
Instead of ice-cold emotions that blur

Lines of love, lines of hope
No need for us to sit and mope
Instead of loyalty to show love and affection
We just sit and think of past reflection

THE PRISONER OF LOVE

I am the prisoner of love,
Caught inside love's spider web.
Who would you suppose caught my love?
My life, my love, my wife, my Deb.

The prisoner of love is all I am.
I can't control the situation.
Even though I may still get slammed.
I thank God for this great nation.

Free to love, free to voice.
Free to marry, and to rejoice.

A prisoner of love, I am to you.
You hold the key, to my prison door.
There's no other thing that I can do.
Because of the love I have in store,
For you my love, I am the prisoner
of love, for life, forever for you.
Never free of the love, my eyes are in a blur.
I am forever a prisoner of love, to you!

YOU DON'T LOVE ME

You don't love me---you know it's a lie.
If you had just one wish for me---it would be for me to die.
You might think I'm kidding---maybe just a little bit.
But ever since the wedding day---you've made me feel like s*it.

You pretend to support me,
with all of my dreams.
But when they don't work out overnight it seems,
you always turn your back on me.

You might think I'm exaggerating,
or just telling one side of the story.
But it seems like you're always complaining,
about everything I do whether exciting or boring.

I can never please you---no matter what I do.
So I'm not even going to try---I'd rather just die.

Call it a copout ---call it what you will.
Sometimes I get so angry ---all I want to do is kill,
myself, or you or anyone in my way.
I guess what I should do is just kneel down and pray.

Pray for some patience---pray for some strength.
Pray to end my negligence,
of anger disguised as strength.

I'm afraid too much patience---won't let me be me.
God don't give me too much patience---or I'll loose my individuality.

Being different is real important to me.
There's no one else on this planet that I would rather be.

God please give me strength to carry on,
just one more day to sing just one more song.

YOU GIVE MEANING TO MY LIFE

You give meaning to my life
I thank God for you, my wife
You give meaning to the love
I have for you, from up above

You give meaning to my life
Even though you cause a lot of strife
You're still my one and only love
More precious than a little white dove

You are the reason for me to live
My reason for love,
My reason to give
If not for you,
I would have no life
I thank God again
For sending such a beautiful wife
For me to love,
For me to enjoy
For giving me a daughter
And a couple of boys

ANXIETY AND DEPRESSION

Anxiety. Loneliness.
Depression. Despair.
Feelings of worthlessness,
are always in the air,
causing so much laziness,
 you just cannot bare.
The feelings you get,
 you need to get out and share,
or else they will eat you up,
 down to your core.
There will be no more room,
 for the feelings to be stored.

One day soon, you can't take it any more.
If you had a gun, you'd pull the trigger,
and be laying on the floor,
in a big puddle of your own blood, warm and red.
No more depression now that you are dead.

Now you deal with God, and what he has said,
throughout the Bible, that you know you have not read.
It's too late now---to accept Jesus as lord,
and savior of your life now---that you have broken the chord,
of life that you had.
Now everyone is sad.
You had so much to live for.
Now your family deals with the funerals chore.

CALL ME LAZY

Call me lazy,
call me what you will,
but life is way too crazy,
waking up with a ginseng pill.

I feel so tired and all alone,
no one to talk to on the telephone.
I'll just sit here and sleep some more,
no where to go if I walk outside the door.

I can't help the feelings that I get,
when I wake up in the morning, I just let,
my body roll over, and my eyes close again.
I don't want to face the world, no not again.

Same old thing, still no money,
another fight, life is not funny.
Nothing to do, nowhere to go,
I'll just sit here and take life real slow.

Try not to rush; I'll get swept away,
I won't have the strength to face another day.
Call me lazy, I've said it before,
depression is my illness, leaking from my mind's backdoor.

CAN YOU RELATE

Pain! Agony! Misery! Defeat!
There is nobody, on this planet you can't beat.

Deception! Despair! Disastrous Decisions!
Stay strong; don't give in to those temptations.

Lying! Cheating! Stealing! Murder!
After so much TV, all of these become such a blur.

What is reality? What is fake?
I can't handle this; I'll go fishing at the lake.
Temporary insanity, forever it will seem.
Temptations of suicide,
like salmon, swimming up the stream.

Will it ever end, the feelings that you get?
While sitting all alone, sad and happiness just met.
Can they get along; will they just fight?

Which one will win? This war is quite a sight.

Does any of this make sense; can you relate?
We all must learn to love, and forget how to hate.

CAN'T STOP

Once I get started,
I just cannot stop.
Thoughts they are diverted,
my brain wants to pop.

Once I get to writing,
I don't know what to say.
It seems to flow like lightning,
then it feels like play.

One right after the other,
they seem to just come out.
I hope it's not a bother,
these thoughts I have to spout.

From my brain, to the paper,
line after line.
Out of thin air, just like vapor,
happens all the time.

Don't know how,
don't know why,
don't even think,
I really try.

Not too hard,
not too easy;
full of lard,
but not too sleazy.

CAN'T HELP IT

Why try to fight it---let the words flow
Can't try to hide it---no matter where I go
Can't help but write it---no matter how slow
Just want to slide it---let the pen and paper show

All my emotion---all of my energy
All of the commotions---inside of me
All of the attention---trying to break free
Moving in different directions---until I cannot see

All of the love---I always try to send
If helped from above---what do you recommend?
If you were the glove---I would be the hand
The separation of---my emotion you always bend

Inside of me---I'll show you who I am
Just like a tree---my roots will always cram
Hope you one-day see---I'm your sacrificial lamb
No one else can be---your ever-loving man

CAN'T SLEEP

Don't want to sleep,
but can't stay awake.
I want to weep,
but there's too much at stake.

I want to hide,
but still be seen.
I try to slide,
but I'm still too mean.

I try not to rhyme,
but I just can't help it.
I don't have the time,
but my brains already lit.

All these words
are trying to escape.
Breaking free from the walls
of my minds landscape.

I guess I can't stop it,
these words are just flowing.
Once I start to commit
the words just start glowing.

DEPRESSION

Anxiety and depression,
are things I know too well.
My life is full of aggression.
I can only begin to tell,
of all the pain and misery,
running through my veins.
I won't let it be a mystery.
I'll let you control my reins.

Feelings of worthlessness,
seem to permeate --- every cell of my body.
Feelings of helplessness,
deteriorate --- my mind, soul, and body.

I can't control this rage,
filling me up inside.
It's like I'm in a cage,
looking towards the outside.

Put me out of my misery --- before it's too late.
Uncover the mystery --- I'll soon be at heaven's gate.

Waiting to enter --- maybe they'll let me in.
To look back at the life I've led,
hopefully it wasn't all wasted.
End this banter --- then my new life will begin.
My old self will have fled.
My soul escaping being basted.

Too many deadlines never an extension.
When will it ever end?
Pressure pushing towards each dimension,
with my mind constantly on a bend.

Open my eyes --- then I will see.
Nothing but a nightmare.
What a surprise --- would you believe?
Waking up is such a scare.

SENSITIZATION

Desensitization---to sex violence and love
Desensitization---to all of the above
Do you know when--- you are desensitized
It's when no matter what happens--- you're not even surprised

Rock lyrics and violence--- will it ever end?
Will they ever silence--- will they ever send
Positive role models--- into the world today
So our children can grow up in safety--- no matter where they play

Television and movies---you know are here to stay
Have they gone too far---or is it just because of the pay
The amounts of money--- which some people make
No wonder they don't care--- about what is at stake

The entertainment business--- complete as a whole
What can be done about it--- is anyone in control?
Will history repeat itself---will we come to an end?
Like previous society's--- that became dust in the wind

Can we learn from past cultures mistakes?
Or is it too late to slam on the brakes?
Should we not worry about all of the gloom?
Is it too late to prevent any of this doom?

DISORGANIZATION

DISORGANIZATION is how I've always been
Some, like my wife think that it's a sin
Don't know how long, don't know how or when
Don't know anything, except this is how I've always been

DISORGANIZATION, story of my life
Can't remember anything, except for all the strife
Constantly fighting over money, with my little wife
The memories cut through my brain, like a double bladed knife

DISORGANIZATION, I think it is just me
Doesn't matter where I am, or even what I see
I don't think I have a choice, don't you agree
Maybe it's just a side effect of stress disability

DISORGANIZATION, nothing matters at all
Every single day of life, problems a mile tall
Overloaded thoughts, slowing my brain down to a crawl
Just a matter of time, before I give in and fall

FORGIVENESS

Forgiveness is something people tell me I should do.
Forgiveness is something; I do not want to do
If I forgive all those who have hurt me,
then I'm afraid I will lose all the pain and misery,
that drives me, and helps me, do the things I do.
Without it, I don't know what else I would do.

I have been told, to forgive your enemy.
I do not believe that would help me.
Maybe it would, maybe it won't.
No matter how much you try to convince me, I still don't.

I receive my strength from all of the anger,
hostility, and hatred that always seem to linger.
I don't want to give up that feeling, that I feel so much.
I guess I like the feeling, because it is such,
a feeling of power, that no one can control.
It is so overwhelming; I think I'm on a roll.

I'm not saying that you should not forgive.
I'm just saying if I do, I don't think I could live,
another day with myself, knowing they got away with it.
Keeping the anger inside, still helps a little bit.

Maybe it is healthy, and maybe it is not.
I really don't care, because I like to hate a lot.
I know it is wrong, but I still do not care.
All I need to know, is the anger is still there.

Keeping me company, day after day.
Being my best friend, when I don't know what to say.
Driving me to strive, to be my very best.
No matter where I am, North, South, East, or West.

FREEDOM OF SPEECH

Freedom of speech is what we are all entitled to,
To speak our mind, whether our views are false or true.
As long as we live in America we are forever free,
This is the way, forever it should be.

You may not like, the words others write,
The words that seem to hurt, while others might excite.
But as long as we are free, no one can ever control,
These words are protected, for all us writers as a whole.

Freedom of expression, feelings into words,
Sentences and paragraphs even if they seem absurd.
Violent, vulgar, or racist the words are still the same,
Forever free, whether they make sense or are lame.

Two sides of the story, whatever words you read,
They sometimes have two meanings depending on your creed.
To some they are racist; to others it's just the way they speak,
So if you don't like them when you listen, think before you seek,
For scapegoats and for the cause, of the anger and the hate,
Because it is not in the writing, which are just thoughts, whether bad or great.
Reflection of society, that's the way it will always be.
If government will open their eyes, then they will see,
That music and lyrics are here to stay forever till the end,
And there is nothing they can do about it; this is the message I send.

FREEDOM

Psychologists, psychiatrists, how do they really know?
Anxiety, depression, does it really show?

Psychologists, psychiatrists, how can they really tell?
Simply by the symptoms of brains starting to swell.

With overloaded thoughts of suicide and more,
pounding through your minds own backdoor.
Always on the attack, never leaving you alone,
like a mean old angry dog gnarling on his bone.

You try to ignore, the feelings that you get.
Inside your brain pounding, it just won't let,
you relax or even concentrate,
then you can't help but just to hate.

Again and again, day after day,
you just wish there was some other way,
to control your pain and your suffering,
and longing to be free.
Maybe one day,
we can all be free.

GODS CREATURES

Cats, dogs, birds, bees
Flowers, bushes, plants and trees
GOD's imagination to create all of these
For mankind's pleasure will not cease

Rabbits, fish, insects too
Elephants, tigers and kangaroos
Giraffes, lions, rhinos and rats
Whales, sharks, and vampire bats

Butterflies, snails, fly's and worms
Funguses, molds and throw in some germs
Amphibians and crustaceans
Causing many frustrations

Seashells and the creatures that used to live in them
Squirrels, gophers and beavers building a new dam
Grass, weeds, rocks and sand
Any one of these can be quite grand

To view the beauty there is much more
There is no limit to what GOD has in store

HE PICKED THE ROAD LESS TRAVELED BY

He picked the road less traveled by
The road we all must travel by
The choice is ours, will we make it right
Or will we choose wrong and end up in fright
Heaven or hell, right, wrong or the other
Why are choices such a bother?
Whatever we pick, we live with its decision
So when we pick, we better choose with precision
Regrets after chosen, looking back into the past
Foresight in the future, it can become such a blast
Choices and decisions, thoughts of happiness lost
We live with the consequences at any cost
Heaven or hell, when will we be able to tell
Love or hate, happiness up for sale
Every single day, we all will pay
Life is in the balance, whether at work or at play
Different day, different road to pick
Another moment you know you can lick
How many roads have already been taken
Or choices have already been mistaken

HOLLANDS THEMES

Artistic is what I scored the most
I'm not writing this just to boast
I'm not very social I scored almost last
But I hope this poem gives you a blast

Conventional and enterprising scored the very same
Third on the list, the feelings are kind of tame
I'm not very realistic and definitely not social
I'm more of an introvert and very antisocial

Investigative came in second place
It's hard to describe my feelings, they are so hard to trace
Last year when I took this test before
The results are so different; you never know what is in store

Computers are great; I know I'll learn something new
But writing a new poem for someone else to view
Is better than all the knowledge that is now inside my brain
I hope these words don't make me sound insane

Only one year ago I had no idea what life was up ahead
Now I've written over 160 poems, to throughout the world spread
I know this class will help me, if for no other reason
To eliminate what I don't like
And make each new day a brand new happy season

HOW LONG HAVE I?

How long have I been crazy?
And unable to cope.
How long have I been lazy?
I can't believe I've never smoked dope.

How long have I been afflicted?
Is it temporary or forever?
All my emotions are conflicted.
Every thought about whatever.

How long will I be disabled?
And unable to seek a job.
Everyone thinks I am able.
And now they call me a slob.

How long will the pain last.
Thoughts of surrender.
When will the bills be in the past?
Will we ever live – oh so tender?

How much longer before a degree?
Will it really matter?
Will I still remain me?
Will my bank account really get fatter?

How much and how long?
Questions I always seem to have on my mind.
When I graduate, will my brain be so strong,
That I'll stop being mean and truly become kind?

I CANNOT

I cannot think.
I cannot concentrate.
All of these thoughts,
Are much too great.

I cannot focus.
I cannot relax.
All this information,
What are the facts?

I cannot finish.
I cannot start.
Information overload,
Is tearing me apart.

I cannot lose.
I cannot win.
If I will start something,
At least I will begin.

I DON'T HAVE TIME

I don't have the time.
I don't have the money.
I can't help but rhyme.
I can't help, I'm not that funny.

I try to write something new,
each and every day.
There's nothing else I want to do,
there's so much more I need to say.

So many words I try not to forget,
so before I lose them I hope I can let,
the words flow, just like a drinking fountain;
words piling up, higher than any mountain.

I never know when to end.
All I know, is I need to send,
words and stories out into the earth,
In beautiful poems because they are worth,
millions in memories and in smiles;
stretching along for miles and miles.

Thank you God for giving me,
this gift to write and blessing me,
with the gift to rhyme and to tell a story;
I know one day they will make history.

I LOVE THE NIGHT

I love the night
So dark, no sound
A beautiful sight
No one around

A love for darkness outside
A beautiful ride
Peace and quiet
No need for a riot

The night upon me
Makes me feel so free
No rules, no boundaries
Only darkness and trees

So quiet and peaceful
The nighttime is
More than wonderful
It fills me with bliss

No worries, no bills
When the night comes down
So many thrills
And never a frown

I love the night
Much better than the day
Never overcome with fright
It is always that way

I WONDER HOW MANY

I wonder how many poems that I've missed,
because instead of writing, sleep is what I kissed.

I wonder how many poems have slipped by,
through my brain and into the sky,
because I didn't write the words down;
now the thoughts make my face frown.

So many words I miss, if I don't stop and write.
I wish I had more time, to bring another beautiful sight,
of words, sentences, paragraphs and such,
to everyone in the world; there can never be too much.

So next time I feel the words building up,
no matter what I am doing, I'll stop and write until they shut up.
This may seem strange, or real weird to you,
but if you were a writer, you would feel this way to.

I hope I never miss, another poem to send,
because if I do, the opportunity will end,
for me to write one more, maybe the best.
I never will know if I don't stand up to the test.

So from now on, I'll need to stay aware,
and need to stay alert, and welcome the words no matter where.
I am, or what I am doing, and start to writing,
it will be faster than a bolt of lightning.

IF ONLY I COULD

If only I could live all over.
Change the mistakes I've made.
I should've gone to college sooner.
Perhaps then I would be making the grade.

Should've found a job I liked.
Instead of just settling for,
I should've learned to quit without fear,
the moment I started to dislike.
Instead, I've wasted so many years.
My life's been such a bore.

Should've gone to school, before having kids,
and definitely before getting married.
The pressures I'm under now, feels like I'll blow my lid,
and everywhere I go, I feel I'm always hurried.

Should've saved as much money as I could,
instead of blowing it on everything, that I saw.
Everyone told me that is what I should,
but I was a rebel, had to break the saving law.

Should've listened, and should've planned,
for now is the future, and my budget is unmanned.
It could've been so different, now;
instead at 35, starting over and don't know how.

IF ONLY I HAD

If only I had more time to live
If only I had more love to give
If only there were more time in a day
I guess I would have so much more to say

If only we could change the past
If only the love could somehow last
If only I had patience like you
There would be so much more I could do

If only I had more money to spend
Then I would have so much more to lend
If only I had gone to College sooner
Who knows where I would be with that cure

If only I had less bills in my life
Then just maybe I would feel less strife
If only I never had to work again
I hope you don't think that would be such a sin

If only I had a little more imagination
Then all my poems would be the best in this nation
If only I had more joy and happiness
Then maybe I would feel less tense

If only we could change our mistakes
Spend more time fishing at the lakes
Forget the past and only look forward
Never look back, only look toward
The dreams up ahead and never give up
Until we all win our own world cup

IMAGINATION

Imagination – let it run free.
Infatuation – how can it be?
Stimulation – between you and me.
Justification – I know you can see.

Imagination, don't let it die,
all you have to do is just really try,
just like a bird and soon you can fly,
just believe me, why would I lie?

Infatuation, control your emotion,
calm the big waves, in your minds mental ocean.
Soothing the feelings like rubbing on lotion,
halting the feelings and stopping the commotion.

Stimulation, like leaves in a tree,
the same way you feel about the birds and the bees.
Stop now before you cannot break free,
exciting emotions between you and me.

Justification, you know it feels right,
the feelings you get in the middle of the night.
Being without the one you love, would give you such a fright,
you are my love; you are a beautiful sight.

IMMORALITY

Morals and morality are all out of whack
Everywhere you look, in between every single crack
Morals run amuck, it seems nobody even cares
When it comes to good and bad nobody stops and stares

You could be committing a murder; no one would blink an eye
Maybe just a passing glimpse, maybe just a little sigh
But after that, they get back to their life
Everyone with enough problems of his or her own
 -add this to their strife

Pornography and infidelity, rampant through the land
Sex pays, makes millions for the greedy hand
Of the unrighteous that don't give a damn
Why should they, every single day make over a hundred grand

Will we see these people up in heaven? I really don't think so
I'm not passing judgment, it's just as clear as a flake of snow
Then there's gambling, betting on this and that
Poor people getting poorer while the owners pockets get more fat

Tobacco and nicotine addiction, I've said it before
If the owners could see the addicts scurrying across the floor
Looking for just one little hit off a cigarette butt
Then maybe they would get the same feeling I get down in my gut
Every time I see them, no control for their addiction
I despise tobacco owners for giving mankind this affliction

INSPIRATION NOT PERSPIRATION

Inspiration not perspiration,
is the only way to get ahead,
in this life, before we wind up dead.

Inspiration and determination,
not desperation and perspiration,
is all you really need,
if in this life,
you truly want to succeed.

Inspiration and brand new thoughts and dreams,
give life new meaning, like golden sun beams;
shining down on you, giving a reason to live.
Determine in life, where your love, you want to give.

Inspiration from up above fills your very soul.
Helping you determine, and set a brand new goal.
Perspiration is wasted, never appreciated,
turn it into opportunity, even if you become hated.

Don't listen to the critics, do your own thing.
Who will, in the end, be the one to sing?
Don't follow the crowd, set a brand new trend.
Don't be afraid of records, you know you will bend.

Don't have to be the first,
just have to be the best.
Doesn't matter what your thirst,
or whether in North, South, East or West.
Anything can happen, don't give up your dream.
All of the competition, you know soon, you will cream.

IT'S BEEN A WHILE

It's been a while since I've sat and wrote.
It's like waiting forever to clear my throat,
but I know the gift, I have to give,
will be in a book, to forever live,
in a library, or in a bookstore;
I hope they never, give an ounce of bore,
but instead, put a smile on your face,
and your anger, you will never trace,
while you read, another page;
I'll take you to, another stage,
or point, in time, in your life;
the words cut through, just like a knife,
so sharp and true, to forever keep;
you won't even need, to get any sleep.
You'll feel so happy and wonderful,
because the words, will be so cool;
the way they rhyme, and still make sense,
they'll relax you, and make you feel less tense.
This I hope, is what they will do,
stir inside your head, just like some stew;
simmering and cooking, inside your brain,
helping you, to face life, and maintain.
If they do, all I ask from you,
is share what you've felt, and tell someone new?

LET ME DESCRIBE WHAT IT'S LIKE

Let me describe, what it's like to write.
It's like God's finger, touching my brain,
and what comes out, is a beautiful sight;
whether about love, happiness or pain.

Once I start, it doesn't take too long,
after I'm done, I feel so strong.
The release and joy, of another work of art,
from pen to paper, why did it take so long to start.

Didn't start till I was thirty five,
but have written over one hundred forty already.
How many more, can I write while I'm still alive?
I guess there is no end, as long as I stay focused and steady.

It's been only five months, not even half a year.
Many have brought smiles; some have brought a tear.
Some have been put in books, others made into a song.
Some are real short; others are pretty long.

I hope I've written enough, to leave a legacy,
behind for generations, to read, enjoy and love.
That is the one wish, I hope will come to be.
The power, strength and love, I thank God again, from up above.

LETTING OFF STEAM

Letting off steam, is what we all need to do.
Like working out at the gym, or visiting the zoo.
Washing the dishes or mowing the lawn.
Building all these muscles, feeling all the brawn.

Reading a book or watching TV.
Working on the computer, or sailing in the sea.
Riding ATV'S, or even a snowmobile.
Forgetting about life's problems, making them all sterile.

Going to class, learning something new.
Looking towards the sky's wide-open blue.
Taking little naps, throughout the day.
Sitting and writing and thinking of something new to say.

Letting off steam, is not very hard to do.
Just think of something relaxing, then go and do.
No need for something fancy, no need for anything new.
No need to go anywhere, just need to follow through.

Take a deep breathe, let it out real slow.
If you don't, it will feel like your mind is going to blow.
Close your eyes for a second; think of something new.
There are a lot of methods here, pick the one that's best for you.

LIFE CAN BE COMPLICATED

Life can be so complicated
Sometimes it's too overrated
With problems you become inundated
Then you can't help but just to hate it

Life can be so tough
Always brand new stuff
Never smooth, always rough
You never seem to have enough

Life can sometimes be overwhelming
You never have time to sing
You wish your life were just a fling
Instead you wind up with a sting

Life just bit you, what are you going to do
Pack up your kids and take them to the zoo
What is the meaning, does anyone know what is true
Or are we forever to always feel blue

Life always happens to some slow and others fast
Life can be a hassle and other times it can be a blast
Life is in the future and then it's in the past
You can't control who is first to go or even who is last

Life is complicated sometimes you can't control it
Then you try your hand at loving it
When that doesn't work you start to hate it
Before you know it you have wasted it

Don't let this happen, your future is in your hand
If you are not careful your life will end up bland
And you will only watch from the grandstand
But if you are careful you can make it quite grand

LIFE IS SO TOUGH

Life can be so tough
Always brand new stuff
You think it is so rough
Then life calls your bluff

Life is always different
Each day brings a brand new slant
It feels so much the same you rant
And rave on, until your life is spent

Life can be a blast
As long as you're not last
You don't know when it will end
So all your love, you better send
Before it is too late
And you're standing at heavens gate

Life is so much fun
When you learn to live with the sun
You are the hot dog — life is the bun
You are the joke –life is the pun
Miserable for most – wonderful for some
I hope this poem doesn't sound too dumb
I need to write until the day Jesus comes
And takes us all to his mighty kingdom

LIFE

Life it is so funny.
You never know what to do.
The sun it is so sunny,
the sky, it is so blue.

Life can be a beautiful thing,
when we know what we desire.
Life can be one miserable fling,
if our dreams are never on fire.

Dreams can be so shallow.
Dreams can be so meaningful.
What we must do is follow,
so the dreams can make our life full.

Life is so overwhelming,
so much there is to do.
Life can be so demanding,
when the foot fits the other shoe.

Life is so extreme at times.
You never know what is ahead.
That's what makes living sometimes,
better alive than dead.

Life can be so incredible,
you never know what to expect.
Your dreams can be so immeasurable,
no one can ever detect.

Life is what you make it,
this is what I have heard.
Fake it till you make it.
I think that is absurd.

You control your own destination.
No one else ever can.
The USA is a one great nation.
You can have anything that you can imagine.

LIGHT

Light is the opposite of dark,
the X's spot, that gets the mark,
when you flick on the switch from off to on.
The light shines through and the darkness is gone.

The warmth and heat from the sun,
shines down on you, to give you the fun,
from its glare, warmth, power and heat,
shines down on you, from your head to your feet.

You can't help, but feel the power,
of the sun, on us, we are the flower.
Growing new pedals, every single day.
You know there has never been, any other way.

For us to live, without the sun,
you know we all would be dead and gone.
We need the light, the sun, and the heat.
There is no replacement; you just can't beat.

We should appreciate every aspect of the sun,
even if the heat, isn't always fun.
The warmth you feel, gives you power,
to live your life, every day, hour after hour.

LITTLE BY LITTLE

Little by little--- I lose my personality
Every day a little--- more individuality
Lost in a second---being told what to do
Every single moment---what I can and cannot do

I get so tired ---of people running my life
Then I got fired---now I get it from my wife
I wish there could be---some other way
One day I hope you can see---I can't help I'm here to stay

My personality ---do not even attempt
My individuality ---I'll hold you in contempt
If you try to change---just one more day
You may think it's strange---but you will need to pray

Little by little ---I can't take it any longer
Little by little---I hope I can stay a little stronger
Than you or any of my ex bosses
Who always acted like big fat hosses

Why can't everybody ---just leave me alone?
Stop trying to change me ---I feel so all-alone
Why don't you just stop-- and try to help me
I'll let you be you-- if you let me be me

LOW SELF-ESTEEM

Low self-esteem,
makes you want to scream.
You feel you cannot cope,
then there is no hope.

All you do is sleep,
you wish that you could keep,
the memories of happiness,
instead of only sadness.

Deep inside your soul,
you start to lose control.
You just want to break free,
from all this insanity.

Inside of your brain,
you wish you could maintain,
some ounce of composure,
and then you would have closure,
of the pain inside.
Instead you run and hide,
and then you open your eyes,
to life's big wonderful surprise.

MONEY

People always tell me, that money is the root of all-evil,
but I've read the bible, where it says the <u>LOVE</u> OF IT IS EVIL.
I have always wanted to be nothing but rich,
all of my life, don't think I'll ever switch.
From my way of thinking, I just can't help it.
Nothing short of a millionaire, not even a little bit.

What's wrong with money, or wanting to be wealthy?
As long as I'm not hurting anyone, I think that it is healthy.
At least I have a goal if I still don't know what I want.
If I was a millionaire, you could have anything that you want.

It might not take away all of our problems.
But I bet you a million, that it takes care of 99 percent of them.
They say money doesn't make you happy.
Were they once rich, and gave all there money to charity?

I don't think so. All of these dream-stealers,
have nothing better to do, than to become baby-squealers.
Always complaining, because you want more,
rather than live life like them, their lives are such a bore.

They say money doesn't make you happy, how do they know.
Like being broke really does? I don't think so.
If I got to choose, between broke and rich;
It sure wouldn't take a second, for me to switch.

Spending money really makes me happy,
and if you don't think so, try and shop with me.
I would buy you anything, that you ever wanted.
Something I could never do, if we were not granted,
with some money and a blessing, from the lord above.
I would buy you everything to prove my true love.

MORE MONEY

Money, you know, makes the world go around
Getting heavier, each day, you know by the pound

Each day's troubles, you know, will never end
So you do the best you can, then you try to send

All of your love, affection and time
All of your emotions in rhythms and rhymes

Until there's none left, deep down in your soul
Then you become blinder, than a little mole

One day maybe we'll become free
Of all the insanity, inside you and me
Then life can be so easy for you and for me
To face our problems each and every day

Money they say is the root of all-evil
But you know it is the love of it that comes from the devil

They say money won't make you happy
How do they know I think that sounds so crappy

There's nothing you can do without a little cash
I know these thoughts to you sound a little rash

But try if you will, to do anything without money
The only thing you can do is laugh because it is so funny
To think you don't need money to live in this day and age
Try if you think you can you will just end in outrage

One day soon money will end all of our bills
Without the option of it I'd end up on pills
You know it's the same for you and for me
There's nothing you can do without a little money

NEVER ENOUGH MONEY

I never have enough money,
to share with my little honey.
You might think that it's funny.
If it were, it would be more sunny.

Spendaholic, or just love money;
Love to spend, whether rainy or sunny.
Don't you laugh; it's not that funny.
Being broke is like eggs, which are all runny.

I can't go anywhere without spending what I've got.
It doesn't matter, that it's not a lot.
What I do have, I give it a shot.
I buy what I see, no matter if I need it or not.

You may think it's strange, maybe so.
But I can't help spending the money it just flows.
A little bit here, a little there, who knows?
I wish I knew, where it all did go.

I don't keep track; I guess I should.
If I had some paper, maybe I would.
If I had the time, I guess I could.
Keep track of the money, like you know I should.

But I'm too lazy; I guess that's why.
I'll just sit here, and write another lie.
For you to criticize, and make me cry,
and make me wish that I could die.

NEVER LIVED IN THE HOOD

Never lived in the hood.
I don't know the streets.
I'm misunderstood.
I never even packed heat.

What is it like,
to live in constant fear?
What could it be like,
to have a gun stuck in your ear?

I can't even imagine,
what their life could be.
What is right and what is sin?
Most are dead before their twenty- three.

Too many choices,
too hard to tell,
who's going to heaven?
Who's going to hell?

Sex, violence, drugs and such.
Their lives have got to be too much,
for me to handle I guess that's why,
I'm not in the hood, or else I would die.

NEVER TO SURRENDER

Never to surrender
Never to be free
Never to remember
Never to be me

Always in the future
Never in the past
Never to be mature
Always to be fast

Today and tomorrow
Yesterday is gone
Day after tomorrow
Will it ever come?

One right after another
Never to return
Will it be some other,
day just to burn?

Day after day
Night after night
Don't know what to say
After turning on the light

Day after tomorrow
Will there ever be
no more sorrow
between you and me?

OLD SAYINGS

Don't judge a book by its cover,
Or else you will soon discover,
That what lies below the surface,
Is hotter than Satan's hell furnace.

Don't believe everything that you hear.
Even if words come from mouths you hold so dear.

Beauty is in the eye of the beholder.
Some thoughts are hot and others much colder.
Listen to words sometimes-double meanings.
Throughout eternity and all of its old sayings.

Some like rhymes, others not much.
But when I write, I think it is such,
An overwhelming feeling of satisfaction,
Of words from mind to paper at least I took action.

So many in this world never find true joy,
But that is my wish for every girl and boy.
To pick up a pen and find some paper,
Write down your dreams don't let them become vapor.

I hope these words make sense to you.
I know I've given you so much to do.
I hope your mind can handle this collection,
Of rhymes and words and reason for reflection.

ONE DAY CLOSER

One day closer,
you never know how close you are.
One day further,
you never know how far.
Another passing moment,
a single grain of sand.
Forever you thought,
time would be in your hand.

One day closer;
keep dreaming, don't give in.
All you have to do
is start and you will begin.
Don't give up,
You're closer then you think.
One step further,
you are on the brink.

Dream until your dream comes true.
Don't give up; don't ever feel blue.
Happiness is in the future.
it's within your reach.

I don't mean to sound too sappy.
I don't mean to preach

ONE DAY SITTING

One day sitting all alone,
listening on the telephone,
to another salesman's pitch;
at that moment I wanted to switch,
places with them to see how they liked it,
so I could treat them with the same rudeness, just a bit,
then I realized that's just a fantasy,
but it is so close to my true identity,
so I listened in and tried not to give
in but they were so convincing and manipulative,
so one more happy salesman got a commission,
because of stupid ole me not sticking to my mission,
of hanging up or telling them where to go,
instead my thoughts were way to slow.
So I've learned another lesson;
caller I.D. is such a blessing.
You never have to answer, if the caller is unknown,
if it was important, their name would have shown.
So here you have my story of just one call,
and even though it seems real small;
these thoughts I need to write them down,
so you can appreciate how these words seem to drown,
my thoughts in my mind, when I try to sleep,
as if my mind was a meadow, and the words were all sheep.

ONE TWO

One, two---what happened to you?

Three, four---your body lying on the floor.

Five, six---life gave you too many licks.

Seven, eight ---life could've been so great.

Nine, ten---you could've been up in heaven.

One, two, three---why couldn't you see?

Four, five, six---you could've overcome all the licks.

Seven, eight, nine ---you left you're loved one's behind.

Ten again---you should be up in heaven.

One, two, three, four---Satan knocking on your door.

Five, six, seven, eight---you thought God and Heaven could wait.

Nine and ten---you didn't have to give in.

One, two, three, four, five---you still could've been alive.

Six, seven, eight, nine, ten---you gave in and let Satan win.

ONE – TWO - THREE

One-two-three, take a close look at me.
How do I decide, what I want to be.
Day after day, I still don't know which way,
I should go, so I guess I'll just stay.
Dreaming and longing, for something better.
Every single day, my appetite getting wetter,
for more opportunities, to come my way,
so our situation, does not have to stay,
in quiet desperation, and poverty to.
I know there is something, more I can do.
I just don't know, what it is just yet,
but I soon will find it, this I will bet.
One-day closer, than we both expect,
even though still, I cannot project,
what it is, or when it will happen;
One day soon, all our bills will be flattened,
then we'll have no more left
and we can resume, all our dreams that we have left,
in the past, gone and forgotten.
I hope it's not too late, I hope they're not rotten.
All our dreams will soon come true,
and never again, will we feel so blue,
from the collection agencies calling every day,
but we had no money, so we didn't know what to say.
So dreaming every day, till the dreams come true,
this I think, is what I will do.
A dreamer, an entrepreneur, till eternity;
this is what I am, and what forever I will be.

STORY OF MY LIFE

House is in foreclosure
But I really just don't care
I'm too busy with schoolwork
To give it a second thought

My two boys each play baseball
Sometimes at the same time
So then I have to miss one
Then the games are all over

My wife has no emotions
Or affection for me at all
Sometimes it makes me so mad
I wish I could just disappear

So I spend all my time
In front of the TV
And hope to forget about life
And all its responsibilities

Another day at school
More homework to worry about
Not to mention the dishes
The pool, the lawn, the laundry
And any other chores around the house

Life can be so complicated
If we give in to its demands
I choose to cruise through it
Before it runs me down

I don't appreciate the gift
Of what life is all about?
Maybe I'm just another mental case
That will throw it all away

I still don't have a job
I don't know if I have what it takes
Sometimes school is better than a career
Sooner or later I will have to face life head on

SUICIDE IS NO ANSWER

Suicide is a copout.
I have finally seen the light.
I won't let life make me dropout.
Life is such a beautiful sight.

Sent from God as a gift.
If I wasted it he would truly cry.
So I'll let life give me a lift.
And let it give me a natural high.

I won't give into temptation
Of wanting to die.
I won't give into temptation
And end up in hell to fry.

Life is ahead of me
If I will open my eyes.
I'll let life have meaning.
I'll welcome life's surprise.

Suicide won't be my answer.
I will say it one more time.
If any of you are thinking of that door
Choose life as your winning chime.

Life is the answer to your problems.
Death is not the end of the bills.
Your loved ones will be stuck with them
And the misery will take away their thrills.

Life is full of memories
You decide to make along the way.
Choose to make them as smooth as a breeze
Along the ocean of life as if you were the bay.

Life is a blessing live it till the end
With love for your fellow man
And your loved ones hand in hand.
Thank you God for giving me the strength to carry on.

SUNSET BY THE BEACH

Sunset by the beach.
How far can you reach
your eyesight on the horizon?
You'll glimpse something surprising.
Boats and ships sailing along,
looking so big, mighty and strong,
but soon disappearing into the distance.
The ocean causing such resistance
and then from the corner of your eye
you see some whales and dolphins jumping by,
so elegant and smooth, a work of art.
God's beauty in the water is just a start,
then the swimmers and surfers surf on by
cutting through the waves like birds in the sky,
then for some reason you look down at your feet;
Sea crabs scurrying along looking for something to eat.
Sun is almost down; sky is orange and red,
nighttime is upon you, daylight now is dead.
Fog rolls in over you; coolness fills the air,
you've had so much fun today, you almost cannot bare
the thought of going home and back to reality.
You're only wish is for today to forever be
trapped inside your memory always ready to recall,
thoughts of happiness and fun, forever big never small.

TELEVISION

I can still remember watching TV--- over forty hours a week,
back in high school --when I was a skinny little geek.
You may not believe ---but what I say is true.
I was a couch potato---in front of the TV. I was glue.

I remember Happy Days ---and Mork and Mindy.
How can you forget the Jefferson's ---or I Dream of Jeanie?
I remember Sanford and Son ---and What's Happening,
don't forget the Brady Bunch ---and the theme songs we still sing.

I remember Bewitched---and the Courtship of Eddies Father.
How about the Beverly Hillbillies---or Welcome Back Kotter?
I remember Gilligans Island---and Star Trek to.
TV was my babysitter---I had nothing else to do.

Even as a child ---as far back as I can remember,
TV was my best friend---especially the new shows in September.
Even to this day ---I can't break free from the addiction.
I've always loved TV. ---adventure comedy or action.

It doesn't really matter---as long as the acting and writing is good.
It's always been my dream ---to pretend I'm living in Hollywood.
Winning a Grammy an Emmy and of course an Academy Award.
All of these I know I can achieve, since TV never makes me bored.

You've got to have big dreams --- if you plan to succeed.
Try watching Who Wants to be a Millionaire or the rip off show Greed.
The Price is Right is still probably one of the best,
game shows on TV, better than all of the rest.

Today my favorite show is on Fox called Get Real.
Comes on Wednesday night after Beverly Hills.
Of course my other favorite has got to be ER.
And last but not least, WWF Monday Night Raw.

TEN YEARS WASTED

One day I should thank Donna
For being such a witch
I wish she was in the electric chair
And that I could pull the switch
Ten years of my life
Is gone in a moment
Good thing I have my wife
All of the fights that we have spent

Together worrying about money
Without her by my side
There would never be another day sunny
I might not even be alive

It would have been so easy
To go postal on all of them
If only I had an Uzi
To get rid of all of them

I know this sounds real crazy
But I bet you've have the urge
Thoughts of your coworkers who are lazy
The bullets you'd love to splurge

You'd probably never do it
And of course neither would I
But just thinking about it
Puts a twinkle in my eye

I know I need to thank them all
For being such real jerks
Stuck-up overpaid coworkers making me feel so small
Don't any of them know their only library clerks?

Status in a title that's all it's ever been
A degree a little piece of paper allowing them to earn twice as much as me
If you ask me I'll tell you it's a sin
I'm glad they helped me to open my eyes and see
That they are no better but much worse than me
I'm getting on with my life it never would have happened
If not for the experience of my ego that they all had flattened

THE SADDEST DAY

The saddest experience that I've ever had
Has to be Greg's funeral, you can't imagine how sad
I felt, and they felt, we all felt the same
Dead at 36 it was such a shame

What a waste, so much to live for
Why did he crash his motorcycle into that door?
Left behind three beautiful daughters and a beautiful wife
I hope for his souls sake he had God in his life

No one knows why these terrible things happen
Some say God has a reason for everything to happen
I guess we'll never really know why
This beautiful person had to die

Riding a motorcycle through the mountains on a Sunday
I can remember it like it was just yesterday
I had just woken up and my mother in law came over
She told us Greg was dead, his life was over

We couldn't believe it, we were all in shock
Even at the funeral we were still in shock
The church was the fullest I've ever seen
He was the nicest person you could ever have seen

We were all at knotts berry farm two weeks before
My mother in law came over knocking on the door
That was the last time we saw him alive
With his wife and children so happy to be alive

THE SIMPLE CHORES OF LIFE

Another sink, another dish
Needs to be washed and then you wish
You had a maid, who would clean up after you
Because there is too much for you to do
Another room needs cleaning up
But you're too busy to clean the mess up
You yell at the kids, get mad again
Too much noise, you don't know where to begin
So you go outside, and take a walk
Then your neighbor stops you and starts to talk
About nothing important, but you still listen to him
You don't want to be rude,
but you think to yourself when will he end
You head back home, to mow the lawn
Neighbors' still talking, how does he carry on
Finally finished, you go back inside
The house is a mess again; the kids are so fast to hide
From messing and fussing, and carrying on so loud
You look all around; you want to be so proud
But anger takes over, and you lose all control
Start yelling again, anger is taking its toll
Time to shower, eat, and sleep
Memories of today, you will forever keep
Another day, same old thing
Not a single minute to dance or sing
Never ending story. Story of my life
Is it just me? Do we all lead the same old life?

THOUGHTS

Used to have thoughts of suicide,
running through my brain.
Now with you by my side,
they have begun to drain.

Out of mind.
Out of sight.
Never to return.

Foolish thoughts,
Selfish thoughts,
hope to one day burn.

As long as you're by my side,
I think I'll be all right.
But if you should decide to leave,
I don't know what I'd do.

Me and you forever,
till death do us part.
Us and others never,
will we ever start.

Together me and you,
forever till the end.
I don't know what I'd do,
without you hand in hand.

TIME IS FAST

Time goes by oh so fast
----You thought it was on your side
Since you know it will not last
---You run away and hide

Time is everlasting
---So much for you to do
You've got to stop wasting
---All the time that you use

Find some new adventures
---So much there is to do
Build yourself some furniture-
--Or go and visit the zoo

You will never run out of new things
---If you'll open your eyes
Go to the river with its running springs
---The fun may become a surprise

Climb a mountain check out all the scenery
You'll be amazed at all the earths' beauty
Check it out ---then you will know
All you have to do---is get up and go

TIME IS TOO SHORT

Time is too short
So little time
Life is too short
It is such a crime

Life is a play
We are all Gods' puppets
Each and every day
Feeling like some Muppets

You wish you had more
Time on your side
Don't care what is in store
You cannot run and hide

Life's time is up
You can't slow it down
Just like a sharpei pup
Always has a frown

Time is constantly ticking
Into the future then it is gone
You endure life's big licking
Tomorrow sing another song

TIME

Time it is so fleeting---goes by oh so fast.
Going to another meeting ---hoping it just won't last.

Time has been and gone---never to return.
Anger building, and getting strong---hoping to one-day burn.

Time only lasts a moment---then it's in the past.
Hope it was all well spent---before it went by so fast.

Time was on your side---if only for a moment.
Trying not to hide---the moments that you've spent.

Time has come---but now it's left.
Hope for some---burden for who's left.

Time for all---is here and now.
Oh so small---opportunity's window.

Don't let it waste---the time you've got.
If you treat it with haste---then you will not,
have any time---none at all.
Very little time, ---for us all.

TOBACCO COMPANY OWNERS

Tobacco company owners can all go to hell,
for all their lies they continue to tell.
Smoking causes cancer, anyone can see.
All the evidence in front of you, or are you too blind to see?

It can happen to anyone, including you or me.
Nicotine addiction, you cannot break free.
Cancer causing agents, included with every puff.
Second hand smoke, that's the scary stuff.

Everywhere you go, someone's always smoking.
You would think by now, people would learn their lesson.
Can't believe, can't understand, their way of thinking.
Don't they know life is a gift and a blessing?

To waste it on cigarettes is such a shame.
Tobacco company owners are the only ones to blame.
Greed for money, growing to the billions.
Year after year, death toll reaches millions.

Unseen, untold, slow lingering death.
Soon there won't be anyone left.
Innocent victims, some dying so young.
Never to grow up and have some fun.

TOBACCO EXECS

Tobacco execs have got no souls,
for the pain and death, no end to these tolls.
How many people have got to die,
before they wake up and open their eyes?

How much pain and suffering,
has got to be endured,
by the innocent addiction of nicotine,
they add to cigarettes and there is no cure?

Too hard to stop, it's so unbelievable.
People will do almost anything, for just one more puff.
Begging and pleading, almost nonstop;
the sight is indescribable.

Even though smokers know, smoking kills.
They continue, just for the thrills,
of nicotine highs and relaxation;
even though the smoke stinks, and they lose their concentration.

Smoking copouts, of everyone dies sometimes.
Nicotine blinding them, of the facts,
that smoking kills, sometimes it's not them,
it could be loved one's, but they'll still continue.
Second hand smoke killing.
How strong is nicotine?
Tobacco manufacturers know the answers!

TOO MANY PEOPLE

Too many people, on this planet we call earth.
It is time for this planet, to have a new rebirth.
Control the population, before it is too large.
Way too many people; trying to be in charge.

Too many people; roaming the streets today.
There must be some other choices;
there must be some other way,
to release the pressure; the world is in disarray.
All that is left for us to do is kneel down and pray.

Will we ever live, in peace and harmony?
Live together happily, like two lovebirds in a tree.
Everywhere you drive; everywhere you go;
everybody driving, way too slow.
Holding up traffic, always making you late,
then all your emotions, becoming so irate.

Buildings everywhere as far as the eye can see.
As long as people love living close together,
 that's the way, it's going to be.

Billions upon billions; how does GOD keep track?
How does he prevent anyone,
from falling through the crack?

UNCONTROLLABLE

Uncontrollable laughter, laughing at nothing at all
One moment you are happy, the next you can't help but bawl
One moment you can stand, the next all you can do is crawl
One moment you are walking, the next you trip and fall

Uncontrollable anger, being mad at everyone in sight
Loved ones start to fear, you cause unbelievable fright
You know you want to change, you pray one day you might
All your life, I can't believe you've never been in a fight

Uncontrollable crying, you cry for no reason at all
You think your problems are big, but in reality they are so small
You think your life could've been so different if you were six feet tall
You want to give up on life; you're tired of your bills you always have to haul

Uncontrollable yelling, at the top of your voice
Screaming all the time, you only wish you had another choice
If you had more money, you'd buy yourself a Rolls Royce
Then you realize your reason for living, a wife, daughter and two boys

Control all your laughter; control all the pain
Control all your anguish, driving you insane
You can't control the weather, if you could, there would be more rain
So all you want to do in life, is just try to maintain

VANITY

How much vanity and confidence is too much,
if I think I'm a good writer? Why is it such
a hard thing for me to tell just how good I am?
Tell me the truth. I'm not afraid to get slammed.
After writing a poem sometimes I look and say
damn I'm good; Is that so wrong to say?

Some might not be really so great,
but tell me the truth, set me straight.

So far, everyone tells me they are good.
Tell me which ones are bad, don't you think you should.
So I can make corrections and make them so much better.
Wet your appetite for more, make your salivation wetter.
So every time you see me, you'll always be wanting more.
Never getting tired of reading, the next poem I have in store

Please, won't you share, your thoughts with me?
Open my eyes and let me see.
What makes you happy? What makes you sad?
Which ones are good? Which ones are bad?

Half hour went on by, just finished two or three.
The feelings that I get make me feel so free.
Good thing I had a pencil and paper right next to me.

WHAT IS A POEM

What is a poem – do they always rhyme?
Everyone that I write – they do all the time

I don't like – the poems that don't
So when I write – I just won't

Write an unrhyming poem –that doesn't make sense
Everyone of the poems – I write always make sense

They have rhythm – they have rhyme
They have a beat – you can count on all the time

They tell a story – of everyday situations
Never are they gory – accept no imitations

I don't get – the poems that are out of whack
Never will I let – there style on my brain attack

I will always rhyme – because that is what I like
Happens all the time – just like riding a bike

I try to be the best – time will only tell
I think I'll pass the test – I hope they make you feel swell

Every time you read –any moment in time
This will be my creed –stop your thoughts on a dime

Forever I hope they last – whether in a book or in a song
I hope they give you a blast – whether short or really long

WHAT IS IN THE AIR

Death is in the air
I can feel it everywhere
Don't give in to life's despair
When you see its glaring stare

Love is in the air
You know when you don't have a care
When you sit all alone on the chair
Across the room with a soothing stare

Anger is in the air
Poverty has got you in its lair
Together you and your spouse as a pair
Looking across the table with a gleaming stare

Happiness is in the air
Whether at the park or at the fair
It really doesn't matter where
You both are with your loving stare

God is in the air
I dare you to get out and share
His love with humanity, I double dare
Make sure they see conviction in your stare

WHAT ARE WE

We are all prisoners
of our own tormented souls
Every single day
taking their separate tolls

Pushing the limit
to its very edge
Leaning and shoving
 against life's overgrown hedge

Some give up
give in too easy
If you don't
there's so much more for you to be

Breaking out breaking free
what does life have in store
Choose carefully
when picking your final door

WHAT DOES IT TAKE

What does it take to be number one?
To surpass the earth, the moon and the sun
A dream for all to be only first
Never to hunger, never to thirst

Only number one, no need for second-best
Always trying to be better than all of the rest

Reach for the stars, it's never out of reach
Don't settle for the moon, or only for the beach

No need to settle for, don't give in
If you're gonna succeed, you know you have to win

Reach and stretch and try your very best
Then really soon you'll know you've passed the test

Don't give up; don't ever quit
No matter how hard you may want to split
From the competition of life
For if you ever do, you'll live for eternity in strife

Reach until you can't reach any longer
When you're finished, no one else will ever be stronger
Than you, number one, you know you're the best
Better than anyone, north, south, east, or west

WHEN I SIT DOWN TO WRITE

When I sit down to write,
A rhyme is coming into sight.
Even if I don't know what to say,
It happens this way every day.

I don't know when to start,
I don't know when to end.
All I know is that it's not that hard,
And when I'm done, I can't wait to send,
My poem out into this world,
For the entire population to see.
The feelings I get are so indescribably
Great and true, the best I've ever felt.
And I hope I can make a few hearts melt,
With words so simple and true.
Even if the rhymes are forced,
Please don't act so blue.
Be kind in your criticism,
Be kind in your critique,
I think I am cursed with simplism,
And definitely a lot of mystique.

WHO KNOWS WHAT?

Who knows what this life has in store?
For some excitement and others just a bore.
Overwhelming senses they seem so real.
But then reality sets in; you've been dealt a raw deal.

Love and hate intertwined throughout.
Sometimes all you do is scream and shout.
Depression is reality!
Reality is anxiety!

One more day another moment spent.
Who can interpret our writings and what we really meant?

Everyone's an expert at least that's what he or she thinks.
Who knows what effect on us or how close to the brink?

Where are we going? Where have we been?
Who is to decipher between a frown and a grin?

Who knew what this day had to offer?
Put it off till tomorrow today is such a blur.

Wrote another poem even though it's kind of strange.
I'm trying to stretch my mind to its furthest range.

Write about nothing or everything all at once.
Didn't know what to say but feeling like this for months.

WHY I CREATE ART

Why I create art.
Easy question to answer.
Once I get to start,
my mind I cannot clear.

So many kinds of art,
my specialty the poem.
Any subject I think I can start,
to write a really great poem.

I cannot draw; I cannot paint.
If I try too hard I might just faint.
I cannot dance; I cannot sing.
But a brand new poem, that's what I'll bring.

It might be good; it might be bad.
Might make you happy; might make you sad.
Might be too short; might be too long.
But who knows, one day, they might become a song.

I hope I've answered, why I create art.
Sometimes I can't stop, the moment that I start.
It doesn't matter to me whether you like them or not.
I think this is the only art, inside that I've got.

WHY NOT BELIEVE?

UFO'S, Aliens, Bigfoot,
and the loch ness monster.
Is it so wrong to not
disbelieve in any one or all of these?

Who's to say none exist,
critics, cynics will forever persist.
Who needs proof, just believe.
What is the harm, anything is possible?
Information in your mind, anytime to retrieve;
Computer for a brain, nothing is impossible.

Too many stars and galaxies,
to not believe in UFO'S.
Why limit your realities?
You know the truth about UFO'S.

Bigfoot, Sasquatch, the Abominable Snowman,
why not believe, even if there was a hoax.
I don't believe in evolution,
but don't feel the need to coax.

The Loch Ness Monster, why not?
Left over water dinosaurs,
trapped inside a lake, why not?
Who knows, my belief soars.
Anything is possible, I've said it before;
look around your neighborhood ,
what does life have in store.

WHY, WHY, WHY?

Why are we alive?
How do we survive?
So much for us to strive.
No need to take the dive.

Why do we die?
Is life just a lie?
It would be nice if we could fly
Across the beautiful sky.

So much there is to see
In this great country.
It's for you and for me.
Don't you agree?

Look all around
In the sky and on the ground.
Listen to the silent sound.
Is the earth truly round?

Why do we live day after day?
Waiting to give instead of to pray?
Growing before we start to decay.
What more do I have to say?

Why so many questions?
Why not more reflections?
So many misdirection's
Before the resurrection.

WHY

Why is the sky so blue?
Why is the ocean too?
Why is the grass so green?
Why was my boss so mean?

Why does it really matter?
Why don't skinny people get any fatter?
Why doesn't anybody really care?
Why doesn't anybody like to share?

Why do we all live?
Just to take but not to give?
Why do we all die?
Wouldn't it be nice if we could all fly?

Why is there so much to learn?
So much to dream for so much to yearn?
Why is there so much pain,
So much misery driving me insane?

Why are there so many lessons?
Why aren't there any more blessings?
Why do we do the things we do,
When we know we're not supposed to?

Why don't children ever listen?
Why can't they just always glisten?
Always do what they are told,
Instead we always have to scold?

WRITING

I never really knew---how much I loved to write.
Me and you grew---our love is a beautiful sight.

Once I sit down---and start another writing,
I very seldom frown---my senses start to heighten.

These words are so meaningful---at least they are to me.
These words, they are so powerful---I wish that you could see
all the emotion that is inside of me,
then you'd understand what's it like trying to be me.

Maybe it is just therapy---helping me to cope.
I feel so clean and free---better than any soap.

Striving for perfection---knowing it will never happen.
Life is one imperfection---never controlling what will happen.

I never really know---what I'm going to write.
Sometimes I write slow---but usually it seems like the speed of light.

Fifteen to twenty minutes---is usually what it takes.
All of the minutes---are worth whatever it takes.

If nothing else I ever do in my life---I hope I will have left behind,
some beautiful treasures for my beautiful wife--- I hope she didn't mind.

Reading all my poems, trying to critique---maybe one day really soon,
she will start to admire my mystique---and start to praise and swoon.

WROTE ANOTHER POEM

Wrote another poem.
Hope you didn't mind.
Take these words and store them,
deep in the back of your mind.

Hope you really like them,
but even if you don't,
I will continue to deliver them,
even if you won't ---
appreciate the effort and all of the time,
that goes into a poem --- rhyme after rhyme.

Write another sentence ---just a few more lines,
avoiding stupid words ---as if they were land mines.

Trying to complete a sentence,
and hoping that it makes sense.

Trying to make it rhyme,
all at the same time.

Harder than you think, all of you critics.
Trying not to alienate any of the cynics.
Trying to make you happy--- trying to tell a story.
Staying away from boring--- and staying away from gory.

YESTERDAY IS FOREVER GONE

Yesterday is forever gone, never to return.
I wish it had lasted longer, but another day just burned.
The future is here and now, what will we do.
The day is in your hands, do something great before it is through.

Yesterday is but a memory went by oh so fast,
Store the thoughts in your minds cemetery, so they will forever last.
Before they are lost and rotten,
Now the day is over, gone and forgotten.

Yesterday, just like the Beatles said,
Troubles that should be so far away,
Seem so close, and will forever stay.
You only wish the troubles were dead.

Yesterday, can you still remember?
Everything reminds me of that day in September.
Yesterday, I wish I could live again.
Change the decisions that have been,
So instrumental in my life.
Like having children and picking a wife.
Not these decisions, but something different.
More important like what I did and where I went.
Yesterday is just like the movies, scene after scene.
Roll before your eyes, just like the sands of time careen,
Throughout your life's day, and then it is over,
All that is left for us to do is wish upon a clover,
So tomorrow doesn't end in the same way as yesterday.
What we need to do is live as if it was our last day.

TODAY, TOMORROW, OR YESTERDAY

The good times are here and now.
Hopefully we can survive somehow.
How long will the future last.
Yesterday was today but now it's in the past.

What we did yesterday affects what we do today.
What happens tomorrow will be affected by what we say.
Today, tomorrow or yesterday, it is all quite the same.
Every day affects the other. Life is but a game.

Yesterday was good, will today be any better?
Tomorrow will soon be here, your appetite getting wetter.
As each passing second concludes, into the past.
Your wish is for these moments, to forever last.
Yesterday is gone. Your memory slowly lingers.
Like shifting sand, running down between your fingers.

Yesterday is a memory, only time will tell.
Through the sands of time, listen to that bell.
As it rings in your head, about what is in the past.
Make today the very best, it might just be your last.

YOU DON'T UNDERSTAND

You don't understand
The feelings that I get
With pen and paper in hand
My imagination won't let

Me sleep or even slow down
You may get mad or even frown
But I won't stop
Because my brain might just pop

If I don't write
Just one more rhyme
You will lose a beautiful sight
You'll miss a real good time

No matter which direction
North, south, east, or west
Never mediocre
Always trying to be best

Soon you'll understand
If you will absorb them
Listen to the band
Then you can hear them

The words will come alive
Hope to make you feel great
You'll see what is inside
My emotional heavyweight

LONG JOURNEY IN MY MIND

Take a long journey
To the center of my mind.
Thoughts are everlasting
Even though I don't really try.

Across the fields of yesterday
And climb the mountains of tomorrow.
Drive the freeways of today.
Stopping only for a glimpse of sorrow.

For what I should've done
And where I should've gone.
Only regrets are left
Through the landscape of the past.

Flowers and trees all along the way
Friendships that slipped on by.
Rock n Roll and TV
Are the only constants there to see.

Mother nature calling
Showing off all of its beauty.
The sky, the mountains, the ocean,
The deserts, valleys, and forests.

What is left for me to do?
What should I do know?
I still have no idea.
So I'll just sit and write until the day I die.

Depression is a strange disease.
It eats you up inside.
Your mind is never at ease.
All you want to do is run away and hide.

For those who are not afflicted,
You probably don't understand.
But think about your saddest day.
It is like that first thing every morning.

Every day is a chore just trying to wake up.
Eating, showering, and deciding what to do;
You don't want to do anything.
Then your loved ones call you lazy.

That makes you even more depressed
And angry at the world.
Then anybody that gets in your way that day
Adds to your anger.

Whether cutting you off on the streets,
Or just looking at you the wrong way.
Writing is an outlet,
The best that I have found.

I don't take my Prozac.
I'm afraid I'll get addicted.
Even though they tell me I won't.

Opening up is not easy to do.
But is definitely needed.
I hope you all understand now
All my poems that have preceded.

Husband, father, son, writer. Overeducated writer empowered by God, given creativity and energy to write through stress caused by college, family and life. Cathartic writer dealing with life through rhymes in poetry.Some of my poems feel like songs, some are just cathartic, and others range from love, depression, anger, nature, and life in general. Some don't rhyme and some are kind of strange, but all are from the heart and gifted to me from God. To all readers, thank you for buying, reading, enjoying, and sharing. My only wish is for everyone to enjoy at least one of them and share it with another. Remember you don't have to love all of my poems, but if you love at least one, that would be great. Just like rock n roll or county music, not all songs from a band are good, but some are really great. Thanks for reading and please let everyone know about this book.